A NEW WAY of LIVING

A NEW WAY
of LIVING

Understanding What It Means
to Accept Christ

JOYCE MEYER

FaithWords

New York   Boston   Nashville

FaithWords

Hachette Book Group USA
237 Park Avenue, New York, NY 10017
Visit our Web site at www.faithwords.com.

The author would like to acknowledge that the story used in chapter 3,
on pages 11–13, is an original sermon illustration by Dr. Monroe Parker
and is used by permission of Gospel Projects Press, P.O. Box 643,
Milton, FL 32572; copyright 1977. www.childrensbibleclub.com

Printed in the United States of America

First Special Sales Edition: January 2008

10 9 8 7 6 5 4 3 2 1

FaithWords is a division of Hachette Book Group USA, Inc.
The FaithWords name and logo is a trademark of
Hachette Book Group USA, Inc.

ISBN 978-0-446-53583-0 (pbk.)

CONTENTS

Chapter 1

THE MOST IMPORTANT DECISION YOU WILL EVER MAKE

Are you dissatisfied with your life? If so, you are not alone. Multitudes of people are tired, weary, empty, and unfulfilled. Some have tried religion in hopes of finding a solution to the way they feel, only to be burdened with lifeless and unreasonable rules that they couldn't keep. If you have tried religion, it does not mean you've tried God as the solution to your empty, frustrating, guilt-ridden life.

If you need to feel loved, if you need a friend, if you need your sins forgiven, and if you need a future...Jesus Christ is your answer. He is waiting to give you a new life and make you a brand new creation.

If you are not satisfied with your life, you must change something. If we keep doing the same things we have always done, we will have the life we have always had. You need to make a decision, and it is the most important decision you will ever make.

This decision is more important than your career choice, where you will attend college, whom you will marry, how you will invest your money, or where you will live. This decision concerns eternity. Eternity is time without end, and each of us needs to know where we will spend it. There is life after death. When you die, you don't cease to exist, you just begin to exist in another place. It has been said that dying is like going through a revolving door. You simply leave one place and go to another.

Do you want to have a relationship with God here on earth and live with Him for eternity? If so, you need to receive Jesus Christ as your Savior. We have all sinned and we all need a Savior. God sent His only Son to pay the penalty for our sins. He was crucified and shed His innocent blood as payment for our wrongdoing. He died and was buried, but on the third day He rose from the dead and is now seated in heaven, at the right hand of God the Father. He is your only hope of having peace, joy and right standing with God.

In order to be saved from our sins, the Bible teaches that we must confess and acknowledge that Jesus is Lord, and we must believe in our hearts that God raised Him from the dead.

> Because if you acknowledge *and* confess with your lips that Jesus is Lord and in your heart believe (adhere to, trust in, and rely on the truth) that God raised Him from the dead, you will be saved. —ROMANS 10:9

This type of believing is more than a mental acknowledgement, it is sincere and heartfelt. Many people believe there is a God, but they have not committed their lives to Him. God is the Author of Life, and He wants you to willingly and gladly give your life back to Him. God created you with a free will and He will not force you to choose Him. But whether you do or not will make the difference in the quality of life you live while here on earth, and it is the deciding factor in where you will spend eternity when you die.

Have you done a good job of running your life? If not, why not turn it over to the One who created you and knows more about you than you will ever know about yourself? If I buy an automobile and start having trouble with it, I take it back to the people who manufactured it so they can fix it. It is the same principle with God. He created you and loves you very much. If your life is not satisfying to you then take it to Him so He can fix it.

As I said previously, nothing changes unless you make a decision. Do you want to be a Christian? Are you ready to surrender not only your sin to God but your life as well? Are you ready to turn from your sinful ways and learn how to live a brand new life that is lived with and for God? If so, keep reading because there is a life waiting for you beyond the best thing you could possibly imagine. It is available to all. No one is left out. This is what God says about your future:

For I know the thoughts *and* plans that I have for you, says the Lord, thoughts *and* plans for welfare and peace *and* not for evil, to give you hope in your final outcome.

—JEREMIAH 29:11

No one can make your choice for you. It is yours and yours alone to make. What quality of life do you desire to have? Do you really want to follow the example you see in our society today? God's Word says we came into the world with nothing and we will go out with nothing (1 Timothy 6:7). God is the Alpha and the Omega, the beginning and the end. In the beginning there was God, and in the end there will be God. Every person will stand before God and give an account of their life (Romans 14:12). Now is the time to get ready for that. I always say, "Ready or not, Jesus is coming." Get ready now, make the right decision now, because later may be too late.

Chapter 2

WE HAVE ALL SINNED

❧Sin is deliberate disobedience to the known will of God. We have all sinned. There is no one on the earth who never sins (Romans 3:23, Ecclesiastes 7:20). That's the bad news, but there is also good news. We can all be forgiven and made right with God.

> Since all have sinned and are falling short of the honor *and* glory which God bestows *and* receives.
> [All] are justified *and* made upright *and* in right standing with God, freely *and* gratuitously by His grace (His unmerited favor and mercy) through the redemption which is [provided] in Christ Jesus.
> —ROMANS 3:23–24

Jesus has already paid for your sins; all you need to do is believe it and receive it. If you will admit your sins, be sorry for them and be willing to turn entirely away from them, God will forgive you and make you a new person.

> If we [freely] admit that we have sinned *and* confess our sins, He is faithful and just (true to His own nature and promises) and will forgive our sins [dismiss our lawlessness] and [continuously] cleanse us from all unrighteousness [everything not in conformity to His will in purpose, thought, and action]. —1 JOHN 1:9

You need not wait on God to do something. He has already done what needs to be done. He gave His only Son to die in our place because only a perfect and sinless sacrifice could be offered to pay for our misdeeds. Justice has been satisfied, and we can go free through believing in Jesus Christ and by entering an intimate relationship with God through Him. We cannot go to God on our own—we need an advocate. We need someone as a go-between, and that someone is Jesus. Jesus stood in the gap between us and God, the gap that our sin created, and He brings us to God.

Just as a child has his father in him (his blood, his DNA, chromosomes, etc.), so God was in Christ reconciling the world back to Himself. God loves the people He created, and He is unwilling to see them sold into the slavery of sin without providing a way out. Jesus is the way!

Sin Brings a Curse

God's Word says our sin will find us out (Numbers 32:23). Sin brings a curse and obedience brings blessing (Deuteronomy 28). It may appear for a season that a person is getting by with their sin. Their life seems to be as good as anyone else's, but in the end there will always be evidence of the choices they have made.

When we choose a life of sin, rather than a life of obedience to God, we experience misery in our souls. Man is more than a body made of flesh and bones. He is a spirit and he has a soul which is comprised of mind, will and emotions. It is the personality of man. Sinners suffer in their mind. They are filled with mental anguish, and no matter what they do or possess, there is nothing that completely satisfies them. They suffer emotionally. Since they have chosen to run their own lives, they become frustrated and angry (emotionally upset) when things don't go their way. They know nothing of the way of faith. Trusting God—a power greater than themselves—is incomprehensible to them. They never enter rest in their souls because one may only enter the rest of God through believing in Him (Hebrews 4:3).

Yes, the life of sin is a life filled with curses. Nothing good comes from it. This is what God says about the outcome of the person who attempts to live without Him:

7

And I will bring distress upon men, so that they shall walk like blind men, because they have sinned against the Lord; their blood shall be poured out like dust and their flesh like dung.

Neither their silver nor their gold shall be able to deliver them in the day of the Lord's indignation *and* wrath. But the whole earth shall be consumed in the fire of His jealous wrath, for a full, yes, a sudden, end will He make of all the inhabitants of the earth.

—ZEPHANIAH 1:17-18

These scriptures are fearsome, but they need not strike fear in the heart of a sincere believer in Jesus Christ. Those who believe in Jesus shall never come up for judgment or condemnation (John 3:18).

Guilt and Condemnation

Guilt is the constant companion of the sinner. He may do various things to ignore it, but down deep inside he knows his life is not right. Jesus said sinners are unable to escape the guilt (John 9:41).

The Bible is divided into the Old Testament and the New Testament. The Old Testament is just that, it is "old." It represents an Old Covenant, one that God used to cover the sins of the people until the time came for Jesus to establish a new covenant. Through following a system of making sacrifices for sins, the people's sins could be covered but never removed. The guilt was always present. However, in the New Testament, under the New Covenant we have a perfect and final sacrifice which does not cover sin, but removes it completely. It washes away not only the sin but the guilt that goes with it.

Please read the following scriptures slowly and ponder the power of what they are saying. They are all taken from Hebrews 10.

> And in accordance with this will [of God], we have been made holy (consecrated and sanctified) through the offering made *once for all* of the body of Jesus Christ (the Anointed One). —HEBREWS 10:10, (emphasis mine)

> Whereas this one [Christ], after He had offered a single sacrifice for our sins [that shall avail] for all time, sat down at the right hand of God. —HEBREWS 10:12

> This is the agreement (testament, covenant) that I will set up *and* conclude with them after those days, says the Lord: I will imprint My laws upon their hearts, and I will inscribe them on their minds (on their inmost thoughts and understanding),
> He then goes on to say, And their sins and their lawbreaking I will remember no more. —HEBREWS 10:16–17

Let us all come forward *and* draw near with true (honest and sincere) hearts in unqualified assurance *and* absolute conviction engendered by faith (by that leaning of the entire human personality on God in absolute trust and confidence in His power, wisdom, and goodness), having our hearts sprinkled *and* purified from a guilty (evil) conscience and our bodies cleansed with pure water. —HEBREWS 10:22

These scriptures inform us of many very important and beautiful things. The first is that Jesus became a sacrifice once and for all, and there is no sacrifice that need ever be added to His. Under the Old Covenant, the sacrifices had to be made over and over again and yet they never removed the guilt. Jesus became one sacrifice that is good for all time and does remove the sin and guilt.

The guilt is legally removed, but one may still need to learn how to live free from the feelings of guilt. Actually, the new life lived for Christ requires that one learn to live on the other side of their feelings. They can no longer allow feelings to rule them. They must learn the Word of God and obey it, no matter how they feel. This lifestyle of obedience ushers in blessings beyond compare.

Chapter 3

IT IS TIME FOR SURRENDER

You have either already received Christ and have requested this book to help you begin your new life with Christ, or you have been given this book and hopefully are ready to make that decision now.

John 3:16 says: (KJV) "For God so loved the world that He gave His only begotten Son, that whosoever believeth in Him should not perish but have everlasting life."

Let me share a story that will help you understand the power of that verse.

In the city of Chicago one cold, dark night, a blizzard was setting in. A little boy was selling newspapers on the corner. People were inside out of the cold, and the little boy was so cold that he really wasn't trying to sell many papers. He walked up to a policeman and said, "Mister, you wouldn't happen to know where a poor boy could find a warm place to sleep tonight, would you? You see, I sleep in a box up around the corner there and down the alley, and it is awful cold. It sure would be nice to have a warm place to stay."

The policeman looked down at the little boy and said, "Well, I'll tell you what to do, you go down the street to that big white house and knock on the door. When they come out of the door, just say, 'John 3:16' and they will let you in."

So the boy did. He walked up the steps to the door and knocked, and a lady answered. He looked up and said, "John 3:16."

The lady said, "Come on in."

She took him in, sat him down in a split-bottom rocker in front of a great big fireplace, and left. He sat there for a while and thought to himself, *John 3:16—I don't understand it, but it sure makes a cold boy warm.*

Later she came back and asked him, "Are you hungry?"

He said, "Well, just a little. I haven't eaten in a couple of days, and I guess I could stand a little bit of food." The lady took him into the kitchen and sat him down at a table full of wonderful food, and he ate and ate until he couldn't eat anymore. Then he thought to himself, *John 3:16—I don't understand it, but it sure makes a hungry boy full.*

She took him upstairs to a bathroom with a huge bathtub filled with warm water. He sat there and soaked for a while. As he soaked, he thought to himself, *John 3:16—I don't understand it, but it sure makes a dirty boy clean.* The lady came in and got him, took him to a room, tucked him into an old feather bed, pulled the covers up around his neck, and kissed him good night. She turned out the lights. As he lay there in the darkness, he looked out of the window and saw the snow coming down on that cold night. He thought to himself, *John 3:16—I don't understand it, but it sure makes a tired boy rested.*

The next morning she took him down again to the same big table full of food. After he ate, she took him back to the same old split-bottom rocker in front of the fireplace. She got a Bible, sat down, and said, "Do you understand John 3:16?" "No, ma'am, I don't. The first time I ever heard it was last night when the policeman said to use it." She opened the Bible to John 3:16 and began to explain to him about Jesus. Right there in front of that fireplace, he gave his heart and life to Jesus. He sat there and thought, *John 3:16—I don't understand it, but it sure makes a lost boy feel safe.*—(Author unknown)

Now, if you are ready to surrender your life to God by receiving His Son Jesus Christ as the only acceptable payment for your sins, I encourage you to pray this prayer with me. Repeat the words out loud and listen to each of them so they have meaning to you personally.

Father God, I love You. I come to You today in faith asking You to forgive my sins. Jesus I believe in You, I believe You died on the cross for me, You shed your innocent blood for me, You took my place and all the punishment that I deserved. I believe You died and were buried, and on the third day you rose from the dead. Death could not hold You. You have conquered Satan and taken the keys of hell and death away from him. I believe You did all of this for me because You love me. I want to be a Christian. I want to serve You all the days of my life. I want to learn how to live the new life You have promised me. I receive You now, Jesus, and I give myself to You. Take me just the way I am, and make me what You want me to be.

Thank You, Jesus, for saving me. Fill me with your Holy Spirit and teach me everything I need to know. Now, I believe that I am saved, I have been born again, and I will go to heaven when I die. Father God, I am going to enjoy my journey and live for Your glory!

If you prayed this prayer sincerely, you have made the most important decision of your life. No matter how you feel, God has heard your prayer and answered it. You may feel peace or joy, relief or freedom, and you may currently feel nothing at all. Don't let your feelings be a dictator in your life any longer. Believe God's Word, because He is faithful and true to His promises. He said:

All whom my Father gives (entrusts) to Me will come to Me; and the one who comes to Me I will most certainly not cast out [I will never, no never, reject one of them who comes to me]. —JOHN 6:37

God has promised to be with you always, even unto the end of the world. You may not always feel Him, but He is everywhere, all the time. He always has His eye on you and will watch over you with care. He is concerned about all the things that concern you and has promised to perfect them. He has begun a good work in you and He will finish it and bring it to completion (Genesis 28:15, Psalms 138:8, Philippians 1:6).

Congratulations, you have a new best friend—Jesus—the best friend you will ever have. You can talk to Him about anything and everything because He always understands you (Hebrews 4:15). He never rejects or condemns you. There is nothing too big for God and, for that matter, there is nothing too small. He wants you to acknowledge Him in all your ways and invite Him into every area of your life.

You have become a new creature. Old things have passed away and all things are brand new (2 Corinthians 5:17). You get a brand new start.

You will make mistakes—we all do. You have a great deal to learn and have started a journey that will last a lifetime. Always remember that when you make mistakes, God's forgiveness and cleansing is available for the asking. Be quick to repent of any sins and never try to hide anything from God, because He knows everything anyway.

God loves you very much. He loves you all the time. He does not love you more on the days you behave well and less on the days you behave badly. He simply loves you!

Now it is time to teach about a new way of living.

Chapter 4

A NEW WAY OF LIVING

❋As you enter your new life that is to be lived by, with, and for God, you will find that many of His principles seem upside-down from the world's ways. Actually, it is the world that is upside-down and God's Kingdom that is right side up. We are not accustomed to doing things God's way, and at first they may seem difficult or hard to understand.

Baptism

One of the first things you should do as a new believer in Jesus Christ is be baptized in water. Baptism is an outward sign of your inner decision to follow Christ. When a person goes under the waters of baptism, it signifies burying the old life. When they are lifted out of the water it signifies the resurrection of a new life. It is something we do in obedience to God.

And baptism, which is a figure [of their deliverance], does now also save you [from inward questionings and fears], not by the removing of outward body filth [bathing], but by [providing you with] the answer of a good and clear conscience (inward cleanness and peace) before God [because you are demonstrating what you believe to be yours] through the resurrection of Jesus Christ. —1 PETER 3:21

And Peter answered them, Repent (change your views and purpose to accept the will of God in your inner selves instead of rejecting it) and be baptized, every one of you, in the name of Jesus Christ for the forgiveness of *and* release from your sins; and you shall receive the gift of the Holy Spirit. —ACTS 2:38

Going to Church

Another thing I highly recommend is participation in a local church family. Going to church does not make one a Christian any more than sitting in my garage would make me a car. We don't become Christians simply by virtue of going to church, but if we are Christians we should want to worship God and fellowship with other believers. Church is also a place where we learn God's Word.

Not all churches are good churches. Some are religious edifices that look good on the outside, but there is nothing going on inside that will really help anybody. If you attend a church that is not feeding you God's Word and challenging you to grow daily in your walk with God, keep looking until you find one. Churches, like doctors, are not all good; but, they are not all bad either. You just need to find the one that is right for you. Some people prefer a larger church and some a smaller one. Some have one denominational preference over another, and then there are those who prefer a non-denominational church, which simply means they don't belong to a larger organization. The main point is it will help you if you have a solid church commitment. It affords you the opportunity to make friends who are like-minded with your beliefs and to socialize on a moral level that will help you avoid worldly temptations.

Be sure you go to a church where you feel you are growing as a Christian. It is very important for the new believer to learn many things. If he does not learn and make progress, he is in danger of backsliding or going back to old ways.

Small Bible study groups are very beneficial to new believers. In small groups, you will normally have an opportunity to learn, ask questions, receive prayer, and be involved in praying for others. Hopefully, your church will provide adult Bible classes or home groups in which you can be involved. Church is not merely a place to be ministered to, it is a place for us to find and express our ministry within the body of

Christ (the church). Besides receiving from others, you need to give out to others.

Commitment

Being committed is very important. It is not what we did wrong once that got our lives into such a mess, it was what we did wrong consistently. And doing something right once or twice won't help us live the new life God has for us. We must persevere and do what we know we should do even when we don't feel like doing it. We must be consistent. God has given you a spirit of self-control and discipline (2 Timothy 1:7) and all you need to do is exercise it.

Be committed to spending time with God. Study His Word and read books that help you understand the Bible even better. Listen to teaching tapes and CDs or watch good Christian television programming. Take time for prayer. Learn to pray your way through the day. Remember, God is interested in everything that concerns you, and prayer is simply conversation with God. As you grow as a Christian, you will learn not only how to talk to God but how to hear from Him as well, and it will add an exciting dimension to your walk with Him.

Another very important area requiring commitment is giving. God has given us so much that it is natural to want to give back to Him and His work on the earth. When you have been helped, it is only natural to want to help others, and one of the ways you can do that is through committed giving to your church and other ministries that have helped you and in which you believe. Everything we give to God, He gives back many times over. His word says we reap what we sow.

Prior to accepting Christ and becoming a new creature in Him, we had no serious interest in giving. We were selfish and wanted others to give to us, but our heart changes as we fall more deeply in love with Jesus.

Being Baptized in the Holy Spirit

To baptize means to completely submerge. Anything that is submerged is filled if there is an opening in it. If you are open, you can be completely filled with the Holy Spirit. You received the Holy Spirit when you received Jesus as your Savior, but you may not have been at a point where you were ready to open up every room in your heart and let Him completely fill you.

You have the Holy Spirit, but you want to be sure that He has all of you. God wants to use you in His service, and you will need the power of His Spirit to be successful and productive.

God also offers us supernatural gifts (endowments of supernatural energy) to help us live our daily lives. The gifts are varied and everyone receives them, but some may be more dominant than others. I am gifted to teach, others are gifted in music or administration, acts of mercy or helping. There are nine gifts mentioned in 1 Corinthians 12:7–10 that we should be aware of. We are actually taught to covet (seriously desire) these gifts. They are words of knowledge, words of wisdom, the gift of faith, powers of healing, working of miracles, prophecy (interpreting the divine will and purpose of God), the ability to discern between good and evil spirits, the gift of speaking in unknown tongues, and the ability to interpret such tongues.

Even though you may not understand these gifts, I encourage you to ask God to give them to you and teach you about them and their proper use. We see many instances in God's Word of people speaking in unknown tongues (a spiritual language). When we pray in tongues, we are speaking secrets and mysteries to God and we edify and improve ourselves. The Apostle Paul said he wished everyone would speak in tongues (1 Corinthians 14:2, 4–5).

The gift of tongues, in particular, has been a point of division among Christians for many years. Some believe the gifts are for today while others believe they are not. I have personally experienced these gifts in my life and have spoken in other tongues for over thirty years, and therefore I know they are relevant to today's Christian. We need anything that will help us.

Quite often people reject what they have not experienced or what they do not understand. This is a mistake. We should read the Bible and believe what it says.

I caution you to concentrate on the Holy Spirit Himself and not on His gifts. The gifts will come. Some people make more out of tongues or the other gifts than they should. When we go buy a pair of shoes, we don't go into the store and ask for a pair of tongues. We ask for shoes and the tongues come with them. It is the same with the Holy Spirit. Ask daily for more of His presence in your life, and the tongues as well as other gifts will come at the right time.

Seek God's Presence, Not His Presents

God wants to do good things for you. He wants to give you many blessings, but it is important that you seek Him for who He is and not merely what He can do for you. God is wonderful beyond comparison, and being in His presence is amazing. As you seek His face, you will find that His hand is always open. If you only seek His hand it will insult Him. No one, not even God, wants to be used for someone's personal advantage.

Ask God for anything you want or need and if it is best for you, in His timing, He will give it to you. But always remember that, more than anything else, you need more of Him in your life. More of His presence, His ways, His character, His wisdom, His understanding, His power, etc.

God is everything and we are nothing without Him. Jesus said, "Apart from Me, you can do nothing" (John 15:5).

> For from Him and through Him and to Him are all things. [For all things originate with Him and come from Him; all things live through Him, and all things center in and tend to consummate and to end in Him.] To Him be glory forever! Amen (so be it).
>
> —ROMANS 11:36

There Is a Lot to Learn

There is far too much for you to learn for me to share it all in this little book. You will need to learn the doctrine your faith is based on and the foundational teachings of Christianity. A new believer's class is usually offered at most churches, and I highly recommend that you attend one. You will learn that Jesus was born of a virgin. I know it sounds impossible, but nonetheless it is true and it is important for you to understand why. You will learn that it is important to give back to God financially so the gospel can be preached to others who still don't know Him. You will learn about the Trinity, the truth of serving one God, who manifests in three persons:

Father, Son, and Holy Spirit. You will learn about the ministry of angels, the importance of the blood of Jesus, how to hear from God, the doctrine of righteousness, repentance, and a multitude of other things.

Although I cannot share everything in this book, there are some things that I do want to share that I believe are of primary importance to your new life, so let's go on.

Chapter 5

A NEW WAY OF THINKING

❧Learning to think in an entirely new way is of utmost importance. God has a good plan for you and your life, but you must get into agreement with Him concerning it. Satan also has a plan for you and your life, and it is not a good one. The thief (Satan) only comes to steal, kill, and destroy (John 10:10). Satan injects all kinds of wrong thoughts into our minds, hoping we will believe them and thereby agree with Him. It is in this way that he deceives people and finds an entrance into their lives.

Do not be conformed to this world (this age), [fashioned after and adapted to its external, superficial customs], but be transformed (changed) by the [entire] renewal of your mind [by its new ideals and its new attitude], so that you may prove [for yourselves] what is the good and acceptable and perfect will of God, *even* the thing which is good and acceptable and perfect [in His sight for you]. —Romans 12:2

The scripture above clearly tells us that our lives cannot change until our thinking changes. If you want a new life, you have to have a new way of thinking. God has a good plan for each of us, but we will only see it come to pass as we learn the importance of proper thinking.

You Can Control Your Thoughts

Perhaps you are like I once was and think you can't do anything about what you think. That is not correct. You can choose what you will or will not think about, and you should do so carefully. Where the mind goes the man follows. We have all had the experience of beginning to think about something to eat. Perhaps ice cream, a donut, or some other tempting food. The more we think about it, the more determined we become that we must have it. If we think about it long enough, we may even get into the car and drive several miles to get it, only to be sorry later that we ate it and wasted our time and money getting it.

If someone has wronged us and we think over and over about what they did that hurt us, we can feel ourselves getting angry and emotionally upset. Our thoughts affect our emotions and become words that we speak.

The next time you find yourself upset or depressed, just ask yourself what you have been thinking about, and you will find a connection between your thoughts and feelings.

The mind is the battlefield where we fight our war with Satan. Second Corinthians 10:4–5 teaches us that we must cast down wrong thoughts and imaginations and bring them captive to Jesus Christ. That means we should think according to God's Word. Anything that does not agree with the teachings of Christ should be put out of our minds and rejected as a lie from the devil. If your enemy (Satan) can control your mind, he can control your life and destiny.

For example, if you have thoughts of suicide, it is not God putting them into your mind. He wants you to live and enjoy your life. If you have thoughts that you are no good or that nobody loves you, these thoughts are not coming from God because they don't agree with His Word.

Negative Thinking

Be careful about any kind of negative thinking. There is nothing negative about God or His plan for your life. It is better to see the glass half full rather than half empty. Being positive never hurt anybody.

No matter what your life has been like so far, you must have a positive vision for your future. Get into agreement with God and believe that good things are going to happen to you. If you have been a negative person like I once was, thinking positively will take some practice. I had been raised in a very negative environment and always expected trouble or disaster, but then I learned that our trouble can actually come through us thinking negatively.

> All the days of the desponding *and* afflicted are made evil [by anxious thoughts and forebodings], but he who has a glad heart has a continual feast [regardless of circumstances]. —PROVERBS 15:15

The first time the Holy Spirit led me to this scripture, I did not know what "forebodings" were, but I learned that they were negative and fearful thoughts that something bad was going to happen. I also had to admit I was getting just what I expected most of the time, which was trouble. I wanted my life to change and didn't understand why God wasn't changing it, but I finally realized that I had to change my thinking before He could change my life.

Don't be negative about anything...not your future or even your past. Your past can be worked into God's overall plan for your life if you trust God. All the mistakes you made can make you a better and wiser person. You can learn from them and decide never to make the same mistakes again. Don't be negative about your finances, friends, family, the way you look, the job you have or don't have, where you live, what kind of car you drive, or anything else. Develop a positive attitude, and it will help you have a positive and power-ful life.

Don't Worry or Be Anxious

Worry and anxiety are two forms of thinking that are bad. Worry does no good at all, but it can do a lot of harm. Re-place all your worry with trusting God to take care of your problems. Worry makes you look older than you are, gives you headaches and stomach problems, and even makes you hard to get along with. It is not God's will for your life.

Not worrying may be difficult at first because you are ac-customed to taking care of yourself and figuring out what you should do next, but remember that you are now learning a new way to live.

People who don't have a relationship with God may feel they have to worry, but you don't. God is on your side, and He says that you can cast your care on Him and He will take care of you (1 Peter 5:7).

Anxiety means that we are spending today worrying about tomorrow. Jesus said not to do that because each day has sufficient trouble of its own (Matthew 6:34). You will know what to do when the time comes to do it, but you probably won't know until then. God wants you to learn to trust Him. He is never late, but He usually isn't early either. For the new believer, this waiting is difficult simply because you are not accustomed to it. However, after a while, you will begin to love it. Your mind will be at ease and you will be free to live each day fully without worrying about the next one.

Each time you are tempted to worry, just remind the devil that you are God's child and He has promised to take care of you.

The pathway to renewing your mind is found in studying and meditating on God's Word. It is the road to learning the difference in right and wrong thinking. For example, a person might think they have to be poor all their life just because poverty has always been in their family, but you will discover in God's Word that this is simply not true. With God's help and by applying His principles to your financial life, you can break the cycle of poverty and have more than enough in every area of your life. God's Word says that above all else He wants you to prosper and be in health, even as your soul prospers (3 John 2). As you mature in your soul and walk in obedience to God, He will give you every good thing you can handle properly and use wisely.

God will meet your needs, and you do not have to live in fear. If you need employment, you can pray and He will help you find a job. He will give you favor and cause everything you touch to prosper and succeed.

Jesus wants you to have a good life. He wants you to enjoy the life He died to give you. Get knowledge, get understanding, get discernment and discretion. Without knowledge people perish, so cry out for it. Jesus Christ is our wisdom from God (1 Corinthians 1:30). Ask Him to cause the wisdom in you to rise up and enlighten your mind so that you may walk in His ways. "For skillful *and* godly Wisdom is better than rubies *or* pearls, and all the things that may be desired are not to be compared to it" (Proverbs 8:11).

My best-selling book is *Battlefield of the Mind*. I would like to recommend that you read it as soon as possible. Remember, renewing your thinking will probably seem like a battle for a while, but don't give up. Those who diligently seek God will be rewarded.

Chapter 6

A NEW WAY OF TALKING

Words are containers for power. They carry either creative or destructive power. At the beginning of time, when God spoke, He created good things, and we should follow His example.

> A man's [moral] self shall be filled with the fruit of his mouth; and with the consequences of his words he must be satisfied [whether good or evil].
>
> Death and life are in the power of the tongue, and they who indulge in it shall eat the fruit of it [for death or life]. —PROVERBS 18:20–21

Careful study of this scripture tells us plainly that our words have consequences. Some bring good and others evil. When we open our mouth to speak, we need to realize the power of our words. Our thoughts become our words, and that is one of the main reasons that Satan puts negative thoughts into our minds. He knows if we take them as our own thoughts that eventually we will speak them, and that will give him the open door he needs to do his dirty work in our lives.

He who guards his mouth and his tongue keeps himself from troubles. —PROVERBS 21:23

The greatest temptation in the world is to talk about what we see and feel, but God wants us to talk about what His Word says we can have. I am not suggesting that you ignore your circumstances, but I am saying that you can overcome them, and how you talk during your problems has a lot to do with it.

The Israelites spent forty years in the wilderness trying to make an eleven-day journey. They kept going around and around the same mountains, not making progress. They had many problems and one of their biggest was complaining. They murmured and complained every time things did not go their way. God wants us to praise and thank Him while we are in the wilderness of life as well as on the mountaintops. What we say during trouble helps determine how long we will be trapped in it.

This may sound strange to you, but your words do have power. Romans 4:17 says we serve a God who calls those things that do not exist as if they already existed. God sees what He wants to happen and talks about it as if it already happened. To do this, you must see with the eye of faith. Faith perceives as reality what it cannot yet see or feel in the natural. Faith takes the promises of God and acts as if they were true!

If we have a problem and we truly believe God will deliver us, we can be happy now. We don't have to wait until we see a change because we have it by faith. We know down deep inside that God is working on our behalf.

When the prophet Ezekiel looked around, all he saw were dead, dry bones and God asked him if they could live again. Ezekiel replied, "Oh God, only you know." In response to that, God told him to prophesy (speak) to these bones and tell them to hear the word of the Lord. Ezekiel began to prophesy as he was commanded to do, and the bones began to come back together. Flesh and sinew came upon them and they stood upon their feet as a mighty host (Ezekiel 37). What a great example of the power of God's Word.

Speaking God's Word Out Loud

I teach people everywhere to speak God's Word out loud and to do it on purpose as part of their daily spiritual discipline. This has been one of the most important things God has taught me, and I can say that it has helped renew my mind and turn my life around.

The Word of God is the sword of the Spirit. It is the greatest weapon you have to use against Satan. He fears and trembles at the Word of God. In Luke 4 we see a time when Jesus was tempted by the devil. He was in a wilderness, He had not eaten for a long time, and Satan began to put thoughts into His mind. Each time the devil lied to Jesus, Jesus responded by saying, "It is written," and then quoted a scripture out loud that refuted the lie. When we learn to follow His example, we are well on our way to victory.

Are you willing to start paying attention to what you say? If you are, you will find, like the rest of us, you say a lot of things you definitely don't want to have happen in your life. I believe we can increase or decrease our level of peace and joy just by the way we talk. If I am correct, why not say something that will make you happy instead of sad?

Speaking in faith is part of your new life, so get started now. You can say things like this:

God loves me and has a good plan for my life.
I have favor everywhere I go.
Everything I lay my hand to prospers and succeeds.
God opens right doors for me and closes wrong ones.
I walk in wisdom.
I am filled with peace.
I am joyful.
I walk in love.

Something good is going to happen to me today.
All of my children love and serve God.
My marriage gets better and better every day.
I am a blessing everywhere I go.

The list can be absolutely endless. Just make sure that what you are saying is what God's Word says. Getting into agreement with God will open a whole new world to you. It will put God's plan into action, and there is nothing the devil can do to stop it.

Chapter 7

A NEW WAY OF LOOKING
AT YOURSELF

❦How do you see yourself? Your self-image is like a photo you carry in the wallet of your heart. I have discovered through many years of ministering to people that most of them don't like themselves very much. I had a very bad relationship with myself for many years and it was poisoning everything in my life. God loves you and He wants you to love yourself. Not in a selfish or self-centered way, but in a healthy way. You cannot give away what you don't have. God loves us and wants us to let that love heal us first and then flow through us to other people. If you refuse to receive the love that God has for you by loving yourself properly, then you can never really love others.

Is your opinion of yourself based on your performance? For most of us that is the case, and our opinion cannot be good because our performance is not consistently good. We are imperfect human beings and we make mistakes. We want to do things right but we always seem to mess up. That is exactly why we need Jesus. He shows His strength most perfectly in our weaknesses.

You are no surprise to God. He knew what you were like when He invited you into a relationship with Himself. He already knows every mistake we will ever make in life, and He loves and desires us anyway. Don't be so hard on yourself. Learn to receive God's mercy on a daily basis. Get up every day and do the best you can for the glory of God. Do your best because you love God, not to get Him to love you. He already loves you as much as He ever will, and His love for you is perfect. At the end of each day, ask God to forgive you for all your sins and mistakes, get a good night's sleep, and start fresh the next day.

Satan is against you, but God is for you. You need to be on God's side because when two agree, they become powerful. You are precious in God's sight, and you have many talents that will be useful to God. Don't just look at everything you think is wrong with you. Don't just look at how far you have to go—also look at how far you have come. You are a believer in Jesus Christ now, and that is the beginning of everything wonderful in life.

Understanding Righteousness

Righteousness (right standing with God) comes through faith in Jesus, not through our own works. It is a gift of God and is given at the time you accept Jesus as your Savior.

There are many scriptures that back this up. I will list a few for your encouragement:

> For our sake He made Christ [virtually] to be sin Who knew no sin, so that in *and* through Him we might become [endued with, viewed as being in, and examples of] the righteousness of God [what we ought to be, approved and acceptable and in right relationship with Him, by His goodness]. —2 Corinthians 5:21

WOW! What a great scripture! Christ was sinless, yet because of His love for us He took our sin so that we might have a great relationship with Father God. God now views us as approved and acceptable and in right standing with Him because we have accepted Jesus as our Savior. I have to say it again…WOW!

Instead of being afraid that God is displeased and angry, we can stand before Him "in Christ" and know that we are accepted.

For no person will be justified (made righteous, acquitted, and judged acceptable) in His sight by observing the works prescribed by the Law. For [the real function of] the Law is to make men recognize *and* be conscious of sin [not mere perception, but an acquaintance with sin which works toward repentance, faith, and holy character]. —ROMANS 3:20

Namely, the righteousness of God which comes by believing *with* personal trust *and* confident reliance on Jesus Christ (the Messiah). [And it is meant] for all who believe. For there is no distinction. —ROMANS 3:22

Yet we know that a man is justified *or* reckoned righteous *and* in right standing with God not by works of the Law, but [only] through faith *and* [absolute] reliance on *and* adherence to *and* trust in Jesus Christ.
—GALATIANS 2:16

It is important for your spiritual growth that you see yourself as having right standing before God through your faith in Jesus Christ. It is a gift from God. If we always feel bad about ourselves, wondering if God is angry at us, we lose the power that God wants us to walk in. We have authority over the devil as believers in Jesus, but we must stand before God clothed in righteousness, not the rags of guilt and condemnation.

Ephesians 6 actually says we are to put on righteousness like a breastplate. For the soldier, the breastplate covered his heart. What do you really believe about yourself? Can you believe by faith that you have right standing with God? You can if you keep your eyes on what Jesus has done for you and not every mistake you make. You will make mistakes and when you do, quickly repent and receive God's forgiveness. This is the only way we can walk in righteousness. It is not our righteousness that we walk in because our righteousness is like filthy rags, but we can and should walk in the righteousness of God through our faith in Jesus Christ.

This wonderful new attitude you can now have toward yourself is part of your "new life" package as a believer in Jesus.

Enjoying Yourself

You are free to enjoy yourself now, and it is God's will that you do so. Don't base your worth and value on what others say or have said about you. Don't base it on how people have treated you or your accomplishments in life. God thought you were valuable enough to send His Son to die for you, and that is a reason to rejoice.

The Bible teaches us plainly that God wants us to enjoy life, and that is not possible if you don't enjoy yourself. You are one person you never get away from, not even for one second. If you don't enjoy yourself, you are in for a miserable life.

Like me, you are probably different than other people that you know, but that is okay. It is actually something God did on purpose. He creates us all a little different. He likes variety. You are not weird; you are a unique original and have greater value than things that are merely copies of something else.

Don't compare yourself with others and spend your life competing with them (2 Corinthians 10:12). Be yourself and enjoy who you are. You need to change in areas just like the rest of us, and the Holy Spirit will be busy the rest of your life working those changes in you. The good news is you are free to enjoy yourself while the work is in progress.

Chapter **8**

EXCHANGING FEAR FOR FAITH

We all know what fear feels like. It is tormenting and prevents our progress. Fear can make us shake, sweat, feel weak, and causes us to run from things that we should confront.

Fear is not from God. It is Satan's tool to prevent us from living the good life God wants us to live (2 Timothy 1:7). God wants us to live in faith. Faith is the leaning of our entire personalities on God in absolute trust and confidence in His power, wisdom, and goodness. It is the evidence of things we do not see and the conviction of their reality.

Faith operates in the spiritual realm. You are probably accustomed to only believing what you can see and feel, but as a child of God you will need to get comfortable living in a realm that cannot see (the spiritual realm). We don't see God because He is a spirit, but we believe firmly in Him. We don't usually see angels, but God's Word says they are all around us protecting us. By releasing our faith in God and

His Word, we can reach into the spiritual realm and pull out things God wants us to enjoy but are not yet a reality.

Satan delights in calling our attention to circumstances and trying to make us afraid of the future. On the other hand, God wants us to trust Him, believing that He is greater than any circumstance or threats from the devil.

The Bible is filled with great examples of men and women who found themselves in desperate circumstances, and the result was that fear filled their hearts. But they decided to put their faith in God, and they experienced glorious deliverances. You must decide if you are going to live in fear or faith. Even though you are a Christian now, you can still live your life being tormented by fears of all kinds unless you decide to live by faith. You have received Jesus as your Savior by faith: the next step is to learn to live by faith.

> For in the Gospel a righteousness which God ascribes
> is revealed, both springing from faith and leading to
> faith [disclosed through the way of faith that arouses to
> more faith]. As it is written, The man who through faith
> is just *and* upright shall live *and* shall live by faith.
>
> —ROMANS 1:17

As we understand the love of God and realize we have been made right with God through the death and resurrection of Jesus, we find it easier to walk in faith. We begin to trust God to take care of us rather than feeling we must do it ourselves.

Courage is not the absence of fear, but it is taking action in the presence of it. When God told His servants not to fear, He wasn't commanding them not to feel fear, but He was telling them to be obedient to Him no matter how they felt. God knows that the spirit of fear will always try to keep us from making progress in our walk with Him. That is why He tells us over and over in His Word that He is with us at all times, and because of that we do not have to bow down to fear.

Eleanor Roosevelt said, "You gain strength, courage, and confidence by every experience in which you really stop to look fear in the face. You must do the thing you think you cannot do."

Be strong, courageous, *and* firm; fear not nor be in terror before them, for it is the Lord your God Who goes with you; He will not fail you or forsake you.

—DEUTERONOMY 31:6

Only faith pleases God. We receive from God through faith. Therefore, it is of utmost importance for the new believer in Christ to learn about faith and begin walking in it. Developing strong faith is done just like developing strong muscles. You exercise your faith little by little, and each time you do it gets stronger.

Matthew 17:20 teaches us that all things are possible to him who believes. Even little faith can move mountains of trouble in our lives. You have probably spent your life trying to solve all your problems and quite often feel frustrated and disappointed. If so, you are on the brink of a new experience. Now you can talk to God (pray) and invite Him to get involved in everything that concerns you, and you will find that what is impossible with man is possible with God.

According to your faith it will be done for you (Matthew 9:29). You may have lived in fear most of your life, but now it's time to exchange that fear for faith in God. It will take time to learn new ways, but don't be discouraged and give up. Everything in the earth works according to the law of gradual growth. Little by little everything changes if we keep doing what God tells us to do.

Chapter 9

ENJOY LIFE

The thief comes only in order to steal and kill and destroy. I came that they may have *and* enjoy life, and have it in abundance (to the full, till it overflows).

—JOHN 10:10

Jesus died so you could enjoy your life. That does not mean that you will get everything just the way you want it and never have any difficulties. It means that through your relationship with God, you can rise above the misery in the world and share a resurrection life lived by, with, and for God through the power of the Holy Spirit.

God is our real life. In Him we live and move and have our being. Learning to enjoy God will release you to enjoy every single day of your life. Enjoy fellowship with Him. God is concerned about anything that concerns you, and the Bible actually says that God will perfect what concerns you. He is working in your life at all times, bringing you into His will more completely.

Don't be afraid of God in a wrong way. We should have reverential fear of God, which means we should respect Him and know that He is all powerful and means what He says. But we should never be afraid that God gets angry every time we make a mistake or that He will punish us every time we fail to be perfect. God is merciful and He is slow to anger. He is longsuffering, and He knows our frame and understands our weaknesses and infirmities.

If you are like the rest of us, you have many things in your life and personality that need to be changed—and God will change them. But the good news is you can enjoy God and enjoy your life while He is doing it.

The life you have right now may not be the one you want to end up with, but it is the only one you have at the present time, so you need to start enjoying it. Find the good things in it. Accentuate the positive and learn to see the good in everything. Enjoy your family and friends. Don't pick them apart and stay busy trying to change them. Pray for them and let God do the changing.

Enjoy your work, enjoy your home, and enjoy ordinary, everyday life. This is possible if you will trust God and decide to have a good attitude. Keep your eyes on God and not everything that is wrong with you, your life, your family, and the world. God has a good plan for you and He is already starting to work it out. You can rejoice ahead of time, looking forward to the good things to come.

Most people live like they believe they cannot enjoy their life as long as they have any kind of problems, but that is wrong thinking. Don't dwell on the mistakes or regrets of your past. Continue to think about the great new future you have through Jesus Christ. You can enjoy whatever you decide to enjoy. You can enjoy sitting in a traffic jam if you decide to. Remember that I am teaching you a new way of living, and your attitude toward life is a big part of it.

I have finally learned to enjoy where I am while I am on the way to where I am going, and I strongly urge you to do the same. There is much for God to do in your life, and He does not want you to be miserable while He is doing it. Just as babies must grow into adults, Christians must also grow. It is a process that often takes longer than we want it to, but there is no point in not enjoying the journey.

God does not expect you to be perfect today. Actually, He already knows that you will never be completely perfect as long as you live on earth. However, He does expect each of us to keep pressing on. We should get up every day and sincerely do our best to serve God. We should admit our failures and ask for forgiveness for our sins, being willing to turn from them. If we will do this, God will do the rest. He will keep working with us through His Holy Spirit. He will teach us, change us, and use us. You have stepped out into a new way of living, and I believe you will never be sorry. Enjoy God, enjoy yourself, and enjoy the life Jesus died to give you!

A PRAYER OF SALVATION

Father God, I love You. I come to You today in faith asking You to forgive my sins. Jesus, I believe in You, I believe You died on the cross for me, You shed your innocent blood for me, You took my place and all the punishment that I deserved. I believe You died and were buried and on the third day You rose from the dead. Death could not hold You. You have conquered Satan and taken the keys of hell and death away from him. I believe You did all of this for me because You love me. I want to be a Christian. I want to serve You all the days of my life. I want to learn how to live the new life that You have promised me. I receive You now, Jesus, and I give myself to You. Take me just the way I am, and make me what You want me to be.

Thank You, Jesus, for saving me. Fill me with Your Holy Spirit and teach me everything I need to know. Now, I believe that I am saved, I have been born again, and I will go to heaven when I die. Father God, I am going to enjoy my journey and live for Your glory!

RESOURCE RECOMMENDATIONS

I have many resources available that will help you learn and grow in your new life. You can request a resource catalog and one will be sent to you free of charge. I also recommend that you request our monthly magazine, which will also be sent to you free for several months.

I highly recommend my book *Battlefield of the Mind* as well as *How to Succeed at Being Yourself*. I recommend *The Word, The Name, The Blood* as a book that will help lay a good solid foundation in your life concerning what Jesus did for you on the cross and the power that is available to you now as a believer in Him.

Pressing In and Pressing On is a good teaching series available on cassette or CD, and *The Mouth* is a series that will help you learn about the power of your words.

If we can help you with anything else, be sure to call the office, and remember, God loves you and so do we!!

OTHER BOOKS BY JOYCE MEYER

The Everyday Life Bible (hardcover or bonded leather)
The Confident Woman
Look Great Feel Great
Battlefield of the Mind*
Battlefield of the Mind Devotional
Approval Addiction
Ending Your Day Right
In Pursuit of Peace
The Secret Power of Speaking God's Word
Seven Things That Steal Your Joy
Starting Your Day Right
Beauty for Ashes (revised edition)
How to Hear from God*
Knowing God Intimately
The Power of Forgiveness
The Power of Determination
The Power of Being Positive
The Secrets of Spiritual Power
The Power of Simple Prayer

Expect a Move of God in Your Life . . . Suddenly!
Enjoying Where You Are on the Way
to Where You Are Going
The Most Important Decision You Will Ever Make
When, God, When?
Why, God, Why?
The Word, the Name, the Blood
Tell Them I Love Them
Peace
If Not for the Grace of God*

Joyce Meyer Spanish Titles
Las Siete Cosas Que Te Roban el Gozo
(Seven Things That Steal Your Joy)
Empezando Tu Día Bien (Starting Your Day Right)

*Study Guide available for this title.

Books by Dave Meyer
Life Lines

ABOUT THE AUTHOR

Joyce Meyer is one of the world's leading practical Bible teachers. A #1 *New York Times* best-selling author, she has written more than seventy inspirational books, including The *Confident Woman; Look Great, Feel Great;* the entire Battlefield of the Mind family of books; and many others. She has also released thousands of audio teachings as well as a complete video library. Joyce's *Enjoying Everyday Life*® radio and television programs are broadcast around the world, and she travels extensively conducting conferences. Joyce and her husband, Dave, are the parents of four grown children and make their home in St. Louis, Missouri.

To CONTACT THE AUTHOR IN THE UNITED STATES:
Joyce Meyer Ministries
P.O. Box 655
Fenton, Missouri 63026
(636) 349-0303 • www.joycemeyer.org

*Please include your testimony or help received from this book
when you write. Your prayer requests are welcome.*

To CONTACT THE AUTHOR IN CANADA:
Joyce Meyer Ministries-Canada, Inc.
Lambeth Box 1300
London, ON N6P 1T5
(636) 349-0303

To CONTACT THE AUTHOR IN AUSTRALIA:
Joyce Meyer Ministries-Australia
Locked Bag 77
Mansfield Delivery Centre
Queensland 4122
07 3349 1200

To CONTACT THE AUTHOR IN ENGLAND:
Joyce Meyer Ministries
P.O. Box 1549
Windsor
SL4 1GT
Great Britain
(0) 1753-831102